A Let's-Read-and-Find-Out Book™

GERMS MAKE ME SICK!

by Melvin Berger

illustrated by Marylin Hafner

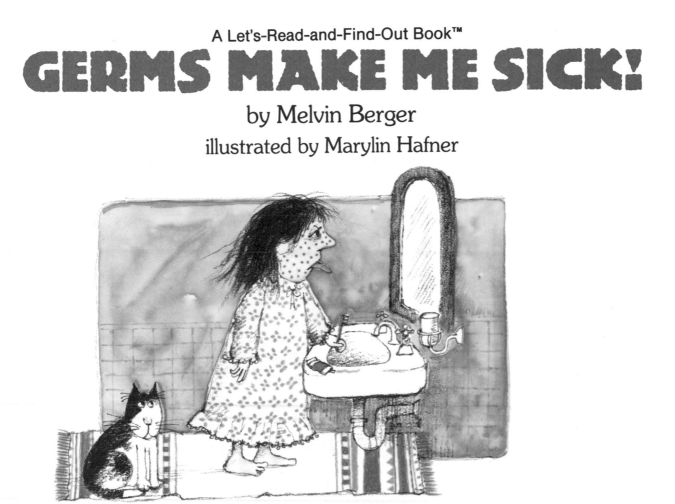

A Harper Trophy Book
Harper & Row, Publishers

The *Let's-Read-and-Find-Out Book*™ series was originated by Dr. Franklyn M. Branley, Astronomer Emeritus and former Chairman of the American Museum–Hayden Planetarium, and was formerly co-edited by him and Dr. Roma Gans, Professor Emeritus of Childhood Education, Teachers College, Columbia University. Text and illustrations are checked for accuracy by an expert in the relevant field.

Germs Make Me Sick!
Text Copyright © 1985 by Melvin Berger
Illustrations copyright © 1985 by Marylin Hafner

Library of Congress Cataloging in Publication Data
Berger, Melvin.
  Germs make me sick!

  (Let's-read-and-find-out science books)
  Summary: explains how bacteria and viruses affect the human body and how the body fights them.
  1. Bacteria—Juvenile literature   2. Viruses—Juvenile literature.   3. Bacterial diseases—Juvenile literature.
4. Virus diseases—Juvenile literature.   [1. Bacteria.
2. Viruses]   I. Hafner, Marylin, ill.   II. Title.   III. Series.
QR57.B47 1985   616.9'2   84-45334
ISBN 0-690-04428-3
ISBN 0-690-04429-1 (lib. bdg.)

  (A Harper Trophy book)
  (Let's-read-and-find-out books)
ISBN 0-06-445053-8 (pbk.)

Colorful Book Plates

Get 28 large full color stickers. Great for identifying your child's books or for identifying other prized possessions. As a gift they will delight any child. To order send $1.00 for each set, plus 35¢ postage and handling to:

**Let's Read and Find Out
Children's Reading Institute
Durham, CT 06422
Markham, ONT L3P 4C7**

Please be sure to include your name and address. Allow 3-4 weeks for delivery.

You wake up one morning. But you don't feel like getting out of
bed. Your arms and legs ache. Your head hurts. You have a
fever. And your throat is sore.

3

"I'm sick," you say. "I must have caught a germ."

Everyone knows that germs can make you sick. But not everyone knows how.

Germs are tiny, tiny living beings. They are far too small to see with your eyes alone. In fact, a line of one thousand germs could fit across the top of a pencil!

There are many different kinds of germs. But the two that usually make you sick are bacteria and viruses.

Bacteria are very much like small plants. But they don't look like any plants you know. Under a microscope, some bacteria look like little round balls. Others are as straight as rods. Still others are twisted in spiral shapes.

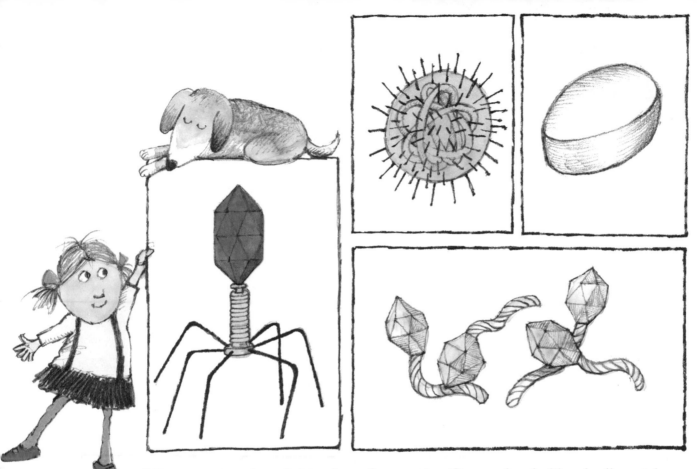

Viruses are far tinier than bacteria. Some look like balls with spikes sticking out on all sides. Others look like loaves of bread or like tadpoles. There are even some that look like metal screws with spider legs.

Germs, such as bacteria and viruses, are found everywhere. They are in the air you breathe, in the food you eat, in the water you drink, and on everything you touch.

Although germs are all around, they do not always make you sick. Many germs are not harmful. Also, your body keeps germs out most of the time.

Your skin blocks the germs. As long as there are no cuts or scratches on your skin, germs can't get in.

Your nose helps, too. It is lined with tiny hairs. The hairs catch many of the germs you breathe in. They push them back out.

The inside of your mouth and throat is always wet. Germs often get stuck there. They don't go any farther.

Yet some germs do slip in every once in a while.

Your friend has a cold. He sneezes. Germs fly out. You breathe the air. Some of his germs may get into your lungs.

You take a sip of your cousin's soda. Her germs are on the straw. A few of the germs may get into your stomach.

You're riding a bike. You fall and scrape your knee. Germs from the ground may get under your skin.

But even when harmful bacteria and viruses get into your body, you don't always get sick. That is because your body has ways to fight germs.

The white cells in your blood go after any germs that
sneak in. Usually, these cells kill the germs before they can do
any harm.

RED
BLOOD
CELL

WHITE
BLOOD
CELL

WHITE BLOOD CELL "EATS"
HARMFUL GERMS.

Your blood also has special chemicals that attack germs. They are called antibodies.

The white blood cells and antibodies don't always get rid of the germs, though. Some germs stay in the body and make you sick.

1 hour

2 hours

3 hours

4 hours

5 hours

What if the germs in your body are bacteria? They quickly start to multiply. Each one becomes two new bacteria. Then they become four, and so on. In a few hours there may be *millions* of bacteria in your body.

The bacteria give off waste products. Some of these wastes are poisons. The poisons can damage or kill the cells that make up your body. When enough cells are harmed, you feel sick.

You may have pains and aches, run a fever, or break out in a rash. You may cough or sneeze, or throw up. These signs tell you that cells are being killed in your body.

18

Some bacteria give off poisons that stay close to the bacteria.
Bacteria in your mouth are like that. Their poison only attacks
your teeth and causes cavities. It does not go to other places in
your body.

Earaches and boils on the skin are also caused by bacteria
whose poisons stay in one place.

Other bacteria give off poisons that move around the body. One kind of bacteria lives in the lungs. But it gives off poisons that are carried around in the blood. These bacteria may give you a headache or a sore stomach.

Still other bacteria have poisons in their outer coats. When they touch different cells, their poisons hurt or destroy them. As the cells die, you feel sick.

What if viruses get into your body? Viruses are different from bacteria. They don't give off poisons. Each virus forces its way into a body cell. It disappears inside. For a while, nothing seems to be happening. Then, suddenly, the cell explodes. Hundreds of new viruses tumble out.

Each virus finds another cell and digs its way in. Then these cells pop open, and more viruses pour out. Soon there are *millions* of viruses in your body.

The viruses spread out. As they do, you feel worse and worse. Viruses bring you colds and the flu, measles, mumps, and chicken pox, and lots of other illnesses.

Though bacteria and viruses can make you sick, you usually begin to feel better after a day or two. Your body has beaten back the germs.

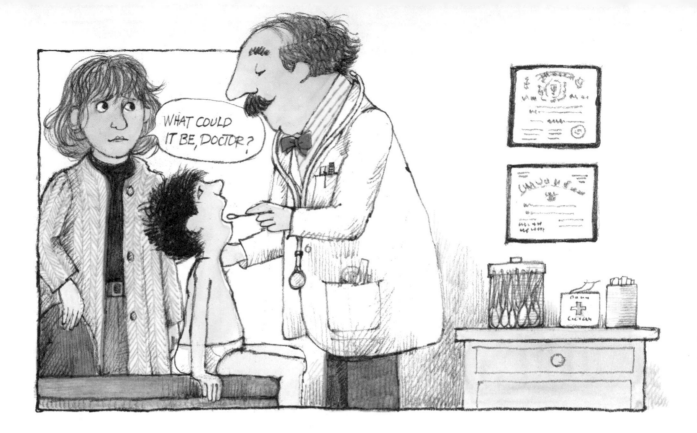

At times, though, you feel *very* sick. Or you stay sick for days. Then you should see a doctor. Doctors try to find out which germs are making you sick.

"What hurts?" they ask. "Let's take a look."

Perhaps they swab your throat with cotton. Then they send the cotton with the germs on it to a lab. Or they may take a few drops of blood from your fingertip or arm. That also goes to a lab to be tested.

Your doctor gets a report from the lab. It tells whether the germs are bacteria or viruses. If bacteria are making you sick, the doctor usually prescribes some drug. The drug will either kill the bacteria or stop them from growing.

Doctors do not yet have drugs to cure diseases caused by
viruses. But they can give you shots to prevent some of these
diseases.

If you do get sick with a virus, the doctor may give you some medicine anyway. It won't cure you, but it will help you feel better. And it will protect you against bacteria that might make you even sicker.

When germs make you sick, your doctor will tell you to stay in bed. Bed rest makes it easier for your body to fight the germs.

29

Once you are well, you want to stay that way.

There are lots of ways to keep healthy.

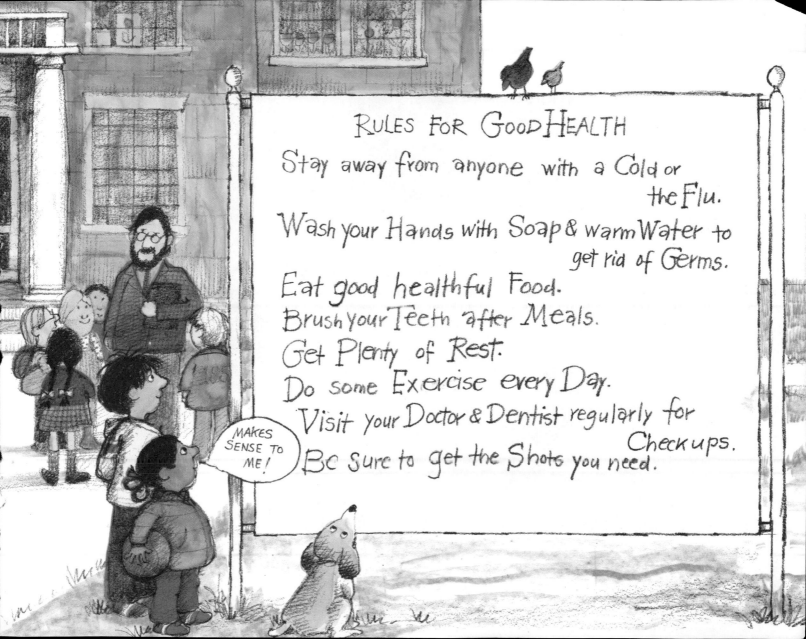

Germs do make you sick—sometimes. But you can help

yourself be as fit as a fiddle all the rest of the time!